CW00702552

Daughters are more precious than one's dreams, however glorious.

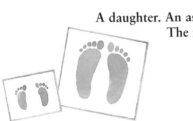

A daughter. An astonishment. A perfection.
The newest thing in the world.
So small.
So packed with secrets.

Daughters do wonderful things, astonishing things, better than you ever dreamed.

Your first butterfly. Your first rainbow.
Your first dinosaur.
Thank you for the chance
to rediscover the world.

Daughters are gifts and spring flowers,
blown kisses, cuddles
and sudden ecstatic smiles.

A daughter is a pile of clothes – a mix of worn and clean. A tangle of tights. A heap of single shoes.

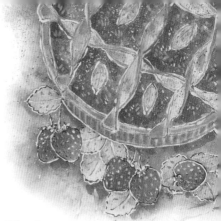

Thank you for an excuse to make
home-made jam tarts... for bringing
back fun to all our lives.

Daughters are a delight. No one responds with so complete a rapture to one's offerings of farmyard imitations, or small surprises.

Life is never dull with a daughter.

Thank you for having given me the chance to make mud pies again, to paddle in the sea, to sail toy boats, to ride the fairground horses.

For daughters the world is full of marvel
that they long to share with you -
pointing to blossoming trees and rainbow puddles

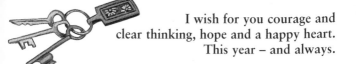

I wish for you courage and
clear thinking, hope and a happy heart.
This year – and always.

I'm proud of all your achievements.
But I'm most proud of your being just you.

A daughter is your part in forever.

Looking back to the day you were born, we smile. How could we begin to suspect the astonishments held in the bundle of blanket?

I loved you the very first second that I saw your face. You are my delight – my never-ending source of amazement!

A daughter opens your heart to all the daughters in the world.

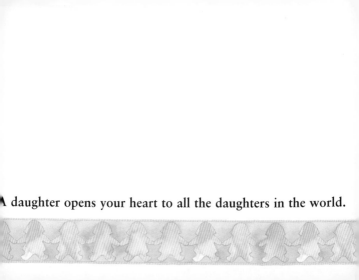

*I will always hold the memories
of your childhood – but will not regret
their passing – for every day
you bring me new astonishments.*

With a daughter, life can never, never never be monotonous.

The best thing you have given me
is your friendship.

I wish you what I have wished
you since your life began.
May you discover what you want to do
– and do it well.

A daughter means that you will know
the meaning of the verb 'to worry'.

*Having daughters is the best investment you will
ever make against becoming bored.*

Thank you for giving me
back young eyes
and a young heart.

Having children is like planting seeds from an unmarked packet ....you get orchids, roses, sunflowers ....all beautiful.

Thanks for all the parcels – knobbly or beribboned,
for all the hurried kisses – smelling of chocolate or Chanel –
for remembering.

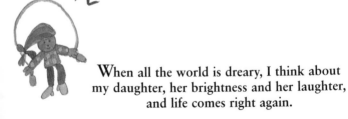

When all the world is dreary, I think about
my daughter, her brightness and her laughter,
and life comes right again.

Through a child's eyes we rediscover the world's loveliness and mystery.

One tiny tug will have me
dropping any masterpiece – you are,
above everything,
the heartbeat of my life.

Thank you for believing
my birthday cakes were magical
my paintings amazing
my stories the best in the world

Be what you want to be.What you need to be
I'll back you all the way
Just be as good at it as you can

*Sometimes when I'm feeling particularly useless
you give me sound advice – which I once gave you.
It cheers me up no end!*

I wish you joy and peace and deep contentment.
And always, always love.

Do you remember spring walks?
Walking by a shining sea and the sound of gul
I do, I do.

Dear Daughter. Take my love with you.
It is as much a part of you as breath.

There is nothing, absolutely nothin
that can cheer up a dismal evenin
more successfully tha
a phone call from a daughte

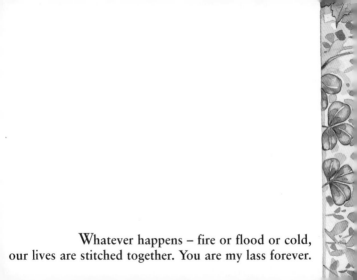

Whatever happens – fire or flood or cold,
our lives are stitched together. You are my lass forever.

Dear daughters –
who have shown themselves
to be wise and good
and kindly and loving.
As in our hearts we always
knew they would.

*My hope for you i[s]
that all your life you will go o[n]
being astonished and delighte[d]
by the world about you[.]*

Do not fear the cold – my arms will hold you in their warmth. Do not fear the dark – I'll light your way.

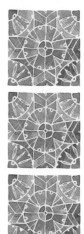

Like it or not, we are bound to one another.
It is the lightest of links....
But it is stronger than life itself.

Here you are, taller than I am,
more street-wise than I am – and gentle too.
Kind. Loving. I am very proud of you.

You have my love – the love that links us.
Take it with you into
the world that I will never know.

YOU ARE OUR GIFT TO THE FUTURE.
A LIGHT, A HOPE, A PROMISE.

There are things I cannot stick together, or heal with a hug. All I can do is be here. Always.

Other Helen Exley Giftbooks:
Daughters...
In Praise and Celebration of Daughters
My Daughter, My Joy

Other notebooks in this series:
Notebook for a very special Dad
Notebook for a very special Mother
Notebook for a very special Son

By Pam Brown Illustrated by Juliette Clarke Created by Helen Exle

Published simultaneously in 2003 by Exley Publications Ltd in Great Britain, and Exley Publications LLC in the USA. Copyright © Helen Exley 2003. Pam Brown, Pamela Dugdale, Marion C. Garretty, Charlotte Gray: published with permission © Helen Exley 2003. The moral right of the author has been asserted.

12 11 10 9 8 7 6 5 4 3

ISBN 1-86187-576-2
A copy of the CIP data is available from the British Library. All rights reserved.
No part of this publication may be reproduced in any form. Printed in China.

Exley Publications Ltd, 16 Chalk Hill, Watford, Herts WD19 4BG, UK.
Exley Publications LLC, 185 Main Street, Spencer, MA 01562, USA.
www.helenexleygiftbooks.com

What is a Helen Exley Giftbook?
Helen Exley Giftbooks cover the most powerful of all human relationships: the bonds within families and between friends, and the theme of personal values. No expense is spared in mak sure that each book is as thoughtful and meaningful as a gift as it is possible to create: good to give, good to receive. You have the result in your hands. If you have loved it – tell others! There is no power on earth like the word-of-mouth recommendation of friends.